You Can See It from Here

You Can See It from Here

Poems by

Jerry Wemple

Detroit
LOTUS PRESS
2000

International Standard Book Number 0-916418-86-3

Printed in the United States of America

Lotus Press, Inc.
"Flower of a New Nile"

Post Office Box 21607
Detroit, Michigan 48221

For Dede

Contents

EPILOGUE

About the Author

Prologue

Story

I.
There is a story I must tell
but I don't have the words to tell it.

Look at me, would you?
Do you know my story?
Will you ask me to tell it?

Speak to me.
Give me your words.
I will return them to you
one hundred fold
but twisted and bent.

Together we will smooth them out again.

II.
I know your story.
It surrounds you.
It is in the manner that you sit there,
legs crossed, only half smiling,
looking away from the light.

The hem of your skirt tells
more than you think.
There's something solemn
in the weave of the cloth
that dangles below your knee.
There is a brittle sadness that lingers,
ever so briefly, about you.
Turn your head and it's gone.

III.
Men carry the mark of Cain.
A tattoo on our souls,
an ink needle-gun drawing

covered up by a shirtsleeve.
We try to hide it
but the mark is indelible.

IV.
This is my story.
These are my words
but they are scrambled.
I cannot understand them.
Let's sort out the puzzle.
Lay the pieces flat on the floor.
Pour some magic whiskey on them
and light them on fire.

I am weary, and wary, and
confused.

Get out of the chair and run quickly.
I am mad and this is all very dangerous.
I apologize; I should not have involved you.

V.
These are the words I do not
have in my vocabulary:

Kindness, Gentleness, Mercy, Forgiveness, Love.

These are the words that I use too much:

Malice, War, Contrition, Sorrow, Anger.

These are the words Paul gave to the Corinthians:

There are in the end three things that last:
faith, hope and love
and the greatest of these is love.

4

VI.
My words are powerful
but I have held them too long.
They have grown weak and bitter,
sealed in a jar with a rusty lid,
stashed halfway down the cellar steps.
Let's put them out in the air.
We'll go down to the ocean to catch some more.

VII.
Here is another story
because I cannot speak my own:
a man washed his hands and,

Using others as witnesses, he said . . . .

I.
KEYSTONE

39

"Campy was the hardest man I ever met,"
Kahn the sportswriter said.

Campy, the guinea-nigger-halfbreed,
Kneeling in a Germantown sandlot
With bruised ribs and a ball in his glove.

Campy rising at 1 a.m. to deliver milk
And two blocks' worth of papers.
Campy who had three grown men pull up

In a white Caddy convertible,
Pay his momma three times
Daddy's weekly wage to let him

Catch games on the weekends.
Campy who quit school at 15. Spent ten
Years squatting in the Negro leagues,

Birmingham to Harlem. Spent ten winters
In the Latin leagues—Mexico,
Puerto Rico, Venezuela—making the year

A hard and dusty perpetual summer.
Campy who got the call from Mr. Rickey
To be fourth, join Robinson at Ebbets.

Campy who slept across town
While the rest laughed it up
And danced a block from the stadium.

Campy who got MVP in '51, '53 and '55.
Campy who had mitts so sore he couldn't
Lift the trophy. Who sat upside-down

In an icy car in a Long Island ditch
Thinking how he couldn't feel his legs.
Who sat upstairs, looking out the window

While his wife made love to another man
In the front seat of a Pontiac.
And Campy who grew old remembering

A September afternoon. And that sound.
And how the ball rose steadily
Just inside the third base line

And how he thought,
"Jesus, sweet Lord Jesus, oh it's good to be alive."

Awl Street

I worked the poorer districts.
The bastards up the hill—with big lawns
And big houses—wouldn't take a thing.

Down in the Front Street river mansions
The old widow women halftimes didn't
Bother to come to the door.

I learned to work the neighborhoods
Where the view was the side brick wall
Of Phelps' Auto Supply, and bent backyard

Fences held nothing much of nothing.
The poor respect the poor. Then again,
Enjoy imagining someone just a little worse off.

Down Awl Street they took it all:
Occasion cards from sympathy to birthday,
September Christmas orders for October delivery

(Printed with choice of greeting and the name
The way you specify). I pitched *The Grit* once
But quit because the premiums weren't enough.

I got my rewards: Cassette deck
When they first came out, a silver
Spider bike with a three-speed gearshift

And a sissy bar.
But you had to do it right.
Act polite, almost shy, especially when collecting.

And they'd act mock-polite right back.
Fake serious and business-like with a boy.
On some Saturdays I could hear the woman

When she turned to whisper, "Henry,
Gimme money to pay the colored kid."
Two Washingtons for a good sale.

A Lincoln if the sister was over visiting
And took an order, too.
God, I loved those folks.

Sailor Boy in the Checker Bar on Maundy Thursday Night

Jimmy Red, the coke dealer's brother,
Is mouthing off to me.
He's thinking I'm trying to scoop
Rosa. Not tonight. Just
A hey to a neighborhood kid.

He's hammering and hammering.
After fair warning I pop
Him with a sucker shot. Catch him
In the mouth, off-balance.

His boys stand up, then the motorcyclers
Get up because their boy
Clever Trevor is my boy, too.

After the ruckus the barman
tells me BANNED FOR LIFE.

A pisser start to a two-week leave at home.

So I walk. Take a leak in the alley.
Then head across Market, give a quick

Wave to who-knows-who headed
Toward the park in a piece-of-junk
Chevy. Drifting down the street I count

The stores. Shaffer's: gone, Linderman's:
Gone, the pizza shop with two stoners.
I cut across the priest's yard, past
The church. But turn right instead of left.

I'm sweating by now so I sit
On the bench at the Community Garden.
No one around in this part of town.
And I say to whoever's listening:
Christ, even the moon looks damaged tonight.

Bitter Bar

The playground fills my eyes.
No hint of the foundation remains.
Just shale, and a patch of grass,

Steel bars and once-bright plastic contraptions.
Next door, the old white stucco storefront
Is now a day care filled with kids,

Perhaps mine. If I'd stayed.
I bought my first six pack there,
Three years underage. Became

A regular: Watched the Friday night
Fights. Last-call love. Made friends
With the local bikers. Huddled

Around the pool table, we'd drink
Rolling Rock. Do shots of apple schnapps
Or ginger brandy. Wait

For the crowd to come in after
The high school game.
Even after I left, I'd return.

Drove straight from Norfolk
The day the ship hit the pier.
Made it in time for four hours

Of drinking, ordering three-for-a-buck
Pony bottles—the Wednesday night
Special—two dollars' worth at a time.

The slide started when Booth, the owner,
Settled down, sold out. Dale, a cousin's ex-husband
(Or maybe they're still married), took over.

He got erratic. Waved his .357 around
One night, then bought the ones too nervous
To leave a round on the house.

From then on, it was only a matter of time.
But once it was that kind of place.
Leaving at 4:41 a.m. on a February Sunday,

The outside lights off and the door barred
From the inside hours before,
I tramped home in the pink-orange dawn.

Passing the bus station, silent in the cold
Early morning, I pulled out my pocket knife,
Cut a *Times* from the bundle slapped down

On the brick platform hours before,
Then gently, ceremoniously, slid a buck
Through the solid brass mail slot

Of the heavy brown door and whistled
Fragments of a half-remembered
Church hymn the last three blocks to home.

There Are Rumors of Other Things

What Spanish Frankie don't know

Amazes us
'Cause Spanish Frankie
He knows it all.
Spanish Frankie done it all
Growing up

Down in Philly.
He can tell how to get back
At those who done you stone cold wrong.
Like the lighter fluid and light bulb
Trick, a favorite of the Germantown boys.

Spanish Frankie got tattoos, too.
One a nasty-ass thing
There on his left forearm—
Two dogs humping with the motto:
"It just goes to show ya!"

Got it down in the Camp Hill youth prison
When he was seventeen.
"Stay away from the dopeman,"
Spanish Frankie always says,
"Or you'll be down the Hill, too."

Spanish Frankie been here four years
Running the corner store
Over on Packer Street.
And his stories
Getting real old.

So now we go over to the Sun Bowl
To play pinball
Instead of hanging out at the store

Eating chips and buying cigarettes
Two for a quarter.

But he'll be back in fine come late June.
That's when he sells those July 4 fireworks,
Two quarter-sticks taped together
Guaranteed to crack the tires off
Some creep's wheels.

Spanish Frankie still got connections.

Altar Boy

I watch her, him, her.
The veil of her hair.
The touch of her knee.
The sweater.
Nicky Agricola on the other side,
a pious bastard missing it all.
But I'm not the only one.
Father Francis Meagher
steps down from the dais
to the red carpet.
Comes to the edge of the altar.
"You are in church to adore God,
not each other,"
he bleats, returns to the homily.

I like it. The heavy
cloth of the black cassock,
white frock. The golden
chalice. The man who
slipped me five for serving
the funeral Mass.
Her face reflected
in the shining bronze platen
at Communion, as I hear
over and over:
the Body of Christ. Amen.

Pennsy Boys in Jersey

We're cruising through Camden
and out of the corner of my eye
I catch a gander of this real bad
looking place called The French Quarter
only Mike sees it too and points
and hits the brakes and wheels
into the parking lot in the broad morning light.
At least we're not underage
for Jersey so we order up
a couple of gin and tonics.
The dancer, who has a face
as smooth as barbed wire,
is giving me the winks. Meanwhile
Mike is trying to put the moves
on some chippee a couple
of stools down, but her boyfriend,
who looks like his name is Punch,
returns from the john and I think
we're gonna get hurt bad.

We climb back into the car
and take the expressway to Atlantic
City. We pop into Mother's because
it's after midnight and this scary looking
biker dude says, "Step right in." Only that
makes me think we shouldn't.
But we do and inside two bands
are laying down sound in Sensaround.
Somewhere toward sunrise
I say good-bye to this chick
who said her name was Mary,
or Martha, or Margaret, or something.
Ten minutes later Mike is winding
through the gears as we race
this excellent blonde in a yellow

Porsche, red light to red light.
As the names of the casinos blur by
I take an apprehensive look
in the rear view, crack open the last
of a six pack, and begin to recant.

Third Street Third Floor Walk Up

Walking out the back door of Finny's
Uptown Bar & Grill I catch a splinter

On the cracked old handrail the bum
Is too damn cheap to replace. I look up

At the apartment house across the street.
I am overcome by a cold and bitter air. How

Did it get to be this time of year?
That used to be her place. That one

Right there. Finny snookered Crazy
Ike again. Waited until he had a good

Jag going and half his pay on the bar.
Then kicked him out for doing the Moonsong

Dance. Her place is pitch black. No plants
In the window hanging from yellow ropeyarn

Holders. No blue curtains with white lace
Trim dirty from coal dust. Nothing.

Ike will wake up in the morning wondering
Where his do-re-mi got to, then drink

On a tab till next Friday. The building looks
dead. It could use some paint. My boots

Scrape cinders into the pavement and the air
Punishes my lungs. I turn, head down the alley

Thinking I might catch up with Riley
playing pinball over at Johnny's Café.

Jesus only knows where she's gone.

An April Funeral in Pennsylvania

In memory of Clarence Rowe

These men only wear suits for two reasons.
No one is getting married today.

Outside, on the stone porch, we stand
Awkward and alone. A few of us smoke

Into the twilight. A woman wipes
Her eyes. A man cleans his glasses.

Inside you stand five feet
From the coffin: *Thanks for*

Coming. Nice to see you
To folks you might remember.

The Masons leave the room
At ten to nine. They return in white aprons.

Speak of the purity of the lambskin,
Brotherhood. *He's built well and*

Will take refreshment in the temple,
One of them tells us as the others

File past, bend low, whisper
A shibboleth in the ear of the corpse.

In the morning, we go to the college.
I buy a book, a pair of shorts.

We linger. Rest against the hood
Of the car. A thin haze obscures

The spring sun and nascent landscape.
In the distance, a farmer plows his field.

The tractor's steady sputter a reminder.
Pretty girls walk across new grass

As the mist of our voices drifts away
Then dissipates.

Two Days After

The car climbs the hill efficiently.
Heading slowly down the backside,
I brake, turn. A sign welcomes me

to Northumberland Memorial Park.
The air is harsh. Winter's cold shrouds
the land. In a few months new grass

will cover the scar of the burial site.
Today it is a patch of pale brown earth
pock-marked by round gray stones:

the kind the potato farmers curse.
How they cry when those stones
break plow points, foul the harvester,

grow too heavy to lift. Buried, they say
around here, pronouncing it "burr-eed."
Farmers—immigrant Germans of one hundred,

two hundred years ago. Names like Shultz,
Oberdorf, Waltz, Haas. Buried. Once
I thought a man was being vulgar.

It was just the way he said "garage."
It's too late for me. I know only
three words of German and have no

use for them. No one is left to teach
me more. No one left between me
and eternity. A month before my graduation

my mother went to a fortune woman.
She sputtered a warning. Said if I joined
the Air Force I'd not be back. I tricked her.

Joined the Navy, sailed on a carrier
watching cold thunderous metal birds
take off and pray their way back home.

I'll not return. Not until I'm ready
for this field in the shadow of a hill
six miles outside of town.

Sunbury

Past noon on Saturday
In the Polka Dot. A place
Flat and broken as all

The rest. A place I once
Had sense enough to wait
Until sundown to visit.

"Her brother is the idiot boy,"
One of them says.
Which one I do not know:

The one who stopped sipping his beer
To check the box score on TV.
The old one with gray teeth, gray

Thoughts. The one moving toward
The jukebox to play the same song
Over again. How does it matter

If it was one or all?
How they shame themselves.
In this lack of grace I know

That I, too, shame myself.
        At 16, I mocked him.
Leaning out of the car window

As he stood as he had forever,
At the light, by the corner,
Across from Shaffer's Store,

Twirling his string. The twirls
A vortex, his eyes focused
On something that I could not see.

I've moved away, come back,
Thought about moving again.
Given the chance and another drink,

I'll talk about it out loud, tell
Myself and you, "Maybe if . . . "
        She comes in here, not regularly,

Just often enough. You know
How the rest works.
Since I've been over for dinner

It's just about.
Shook the old man's hand.
His, too, sort of. Acted

Like I was new, like I didn't
Already know the deal when I've
Seen it every day for years,

Running over and over like
Some pornographic loop
In a quarter booth at one

Of those places out along the highway.
The mother said the mashed potatoes
Were a bit lumpy. They were.

The mother said the roast
Was usually a bit more tender.
I wouldn't know.

They're calling for rain. We
Could use it. Haven't had
A chance to get out yet this year.

The trick is after a while
She is almost incidental.
Her hair, her lips, what

She has to say.
Essence is overcome.
You get on a track.

In a town like this things
Are expected. Ideas get set
In motion, and you go with them,

And it's easy on you.
Or you don't, and after that
Things just aren't right.

A generation or two ago,
He would have been kept
In the cellar, in the attic, or . . .

Rumors are sometimes true.
There's hundreds of them out there
At the Selinsgrove State Center.

Hundreds. Worst cases, they say.
Rumors for them, too.
They kept him home.

After my fifth beer Conrad
Slides over, speaks his piece.
"Something to think about," he says,

Motions for the barman
To bring us a short one.
I know what he's saying

Before he says it. How the mom
And dad are older. How one day, maybe soon
They'll be gone. And then

Where is the brother going to go?
Whose natural responsibility?
It's a package deal.

"24-7," Con says. "A powerful
Burden." I almost convince myself
I might still imagine

The fragrance of her hand.
But I know within an hour
My mind will be made up.

I'll make a phone call, maybe talk
Through the screen door on the back
Porch about a Navy buddy

Who's got a good job waiting for me
In Tennessee, or Texas. I'll be
Back soon, I'll say. And maybe

I will, but not for them. I buy
Another round and motion next
For the pool table. Zeb the bartender

Switches on the overhead Smoke-Eater.
I watch as it sucks up
The poison-smoke stench of a dozen

Boozers on a Saturday afternoon.
For us, it is our own choice that stunts
Our spirit, the decision to maintain

Rather than progress. We shame
Ourselves by degree, until, finally,
We lack the dignity of shame.

Jesse, It's Getting So an Honest Man Can't Even Act Decent in This World Anymore

She was an angel from Montoursville—
Just another mill town, twenty
Miles north of nowhere. I'm the king,
The king of these mill men.
Holding court each night
In the taverns that line tracks.
Waiting for the train hour special
When drafts are two-for-one.

It was a Thursday night, I guess.
No, I know it. She walked into
The Angle Iron Inn like it's someplace
To be. Walked in like the wind
That slides off Shaffer's Hill, gentle
But just enough to make the cornstalks
Rustle on a mid-summer night.
I'm playing the Trivia Whiz

Quiz video, and doing good.
The jukebox is blasting something,
Something somebody stupid played
Like "Baby Love, Baby Love, Baby
Love." I bounced out of the bonus
Round early, turned, and there she was,
Sitting alone, quiet, in the corner.
Of course, what with those Kesslers

And Tim shooting pool in the back,
Sheath knives, and greasy clothes and
Hair, any stranger is wise to be keeping
Close to the door. What was I to do
But go offer a friendly hand? Now
I didn't right off. Moving too fast

Makes you look like a greedy amateur.
At ten, I went over. Convinced

Her to go riding in my truck. Showed her
The river. How when the moon
Shines just right your eyes can
Ride that ribbon of water clean
To the flat, broad Chesapeake.
We went to the Station House
Across the bridge. She was a woman
With class. An angel with some dignity

Come down to the county seat.
Got us a couple of mixed drinks
And relaxed. Took her home.
Didn't even try to kiss her. Just held
Her hand like some pup. Sang her
Name on the ride back like a fool.
Still you know after the mill
Let out the next day all the boys
Were down here jazzing me,

Saying I got lucky last night.
But it wasn't like that. Yet when
Little Frankie bought me a beer,
I drank it with them. I don't care
If I see her again. She was better
Than I deserve. But tell me how
Do you right a wrong and
Make falseness come undone?

November

Henry,

Time is no longer
on my side.
It has become an indifferent enemy.

Two days pass.
Then three. Then four.
Soon a month goes by.

This afternoon
I looked up
through bare-limbed trees
and saw the white vapor trail
of a jet
thirty thousand feet above.

I almost didn't care
where it was going.

Susquehanna Song

Man, if you gotta ask you'll never know.
                    —Satchmo

Two things I know
and one not well:
You're like a television
my friend's poor mother said to me
in 1970
and laughed at her
off-color joke.

I was born in the shadow
of the slag Susquehanna.
Dunmore town, brown,
black with anthracite,
but sprang (a whisper   hear)
from Baltimore, MD. Me.
Five months in a Catholic orphanage await
till a crooked line crooks my fate.

On an empty acre
of my great-grandfather's farm
a woman cries, sighs.
Can have no babies of her own.
She visits the sister.
Asks for the one who is one too many.
Such a catholic thing to do.
Today, that baby would have been
wiped away.
        A Rose that never grows.

So to the farm I went
and from the window
watched the creek
creep and seep its way

through the valley to the Susquehanna.
Fifth largest river east of the Mississipp.
444 miles long.
From the baseball hall
it flows south, y'all,
to the Chesapeake.
With just a peek at Balmer.

I dare consider to say:
just what father was it
signed the papers on that day?
A twisted give away
Hard to explain away.
Eats at a married man's craw.
Legal? No. I'm legal now.
But not free, white and 21 by a powerful drop.
The old measure cup has holes.
Still flour fills bowls.
Who's ever heard of chocolate bread?
'Nuff said.

I've known the river.
Once in old Sunbury
I saw a Baltimorean look at me.
He sure is dark complected
I said in mimicry.
Christ forgives me.
Sshh, sshh. Don't whisper now.
Say it loud. I'm black
and I'm proud.
But what is Africa to me?
I am the Susquehanna.
Neo-Teutonic pigs' blood flows in my creeks.
Sour Krauts all around me.
Woe is me: not pale.
Too much tale.
Skinny blonde boy: we are all God's deferred children.

Back on the farm
it's a call: two arms,
and plates, and words,
and lawyers.
Bye, farm, bye.
Daddy, we hardly knew ye.
How well do we know anyone?
Drop by drop
I know which way the river flows.
Two branches converge at Sunbury.
Can you imagine that?
I can.
It's not bad here.
My yellow cousin close at hand.
But it's not to be. Mama Rose met another man.
No more Catholic school.
But a strange predicament.

There's black kids here
at Tropic Isles Elementary.
Dark, curly-haired kids who look sort of like me.
Where you stay, they say.
I stay over here and wave good-bye to the bus.

Where's my river? Susquehanna.
Guess I'll have to settle for the Caloosahatchee.
But who's this man
with a step cut block head.
Owns a little sun salt rot house.
Grapefruit tree out back.
Calls it paradise.
The Florida sun glitters
like fool's gold.

        My mother drives a school bus.

Time was. Time was
I'd kick your ass.

There was a time
they did. I hid.
In my room.
I see the world from both sides:
inside out and upside down.
Middle school, middle years.
Part boy, part man.
Part white, part . . .
        red, blue and green.
Mixed
in between the pages of books
and *National Geographic* magazine.
I study culture, love history.
Can't decipher my own.
To tell, do tell
they plea.
I have no answer until I flee the Caloosahatchee.
Go north for one fine-edged summer
with Chuckie, my yellow-haired
cousin. Together we're badder
than a dozen.
Listen to a man called Alice,
dressed in drag,
with young teen malice.
Roam the streets at night
thinking we have happy free will
until Chuck's southern stephead,
drunk, devours our ignorant youth with truth.
Says: y'all are brother.
Each says we'd choose no other.

No one denies
this lie unspoken all these years.
No tears. No talk.
Makes us hate them even more.
One night I walk the railroad bridge.
Toss a stone
into the Susquehanna.

It does not float to Baltimore.
It does not rise.
Remains hidden from my eyes.
But not from theirs.
Or yours.

Return to Florida in a funk.
But this trip doesn't take.
More words.
A plate of mashed potatoes
square in square stephead's snout.
Rose has had enough.
Back to the Keystone state.
She leaves quickly,
later sends a ticket for me:
come for summer, we'll return.
Petty trickery.
Buy, Buy Bicentennial. I fly.
Bye-bye, Noel, my star. My girlfriend.

Hello. Connie Sue.
Sitting on the porch with crazy glue.
Got thumb and finger stuck.
With your long blonde hair and eyes of blue.
There is a sorrow.
Brave me. Pulled those digits apart.
Howja do that? she asks.
Cracks a crazy bubble gum.

Never counted on being no account
in C.S. daddy's eyes.
Pappy says can't be your man.
He don't like my tan.
Refrain. Refrain. Refrain.
To Shikellamy
High I go.
Smoke dope. Hemp. Rope.
Feel the burn.

Out with pain.
Refrain. Refrain. Refrain.

Losing Faith hurt.
Parent's cool, but grandma says
can't be your man.
Don't like my tan.
Refrain. Refrain. Refrain.

Restrain no more.
It's dope galore.
Pot. Pills.
All good thrills.
But really not.
Only a slowly simmering pot.

Chuckie, Chuck. How you do?
Still got a pulse.
Stomach pump.
You're a scarecrow in jeans.
Soon it's off to the U.S. Marines.
No more robin eggs or robbery.
Probation man says
jail next time.
That's worse than school
where you never go.
Say bro', I think we screwed ourselves screwing them.
Screw.   Them.   Anyhow.

On June 4, it's out the door
of good ole SHS.
The cusp of a different reality.
Still time for a wasted summer.
Late August night a girl says to me
I never saw you straight.
Can't relate
to stone-face lying Sour Krauts.

Of course, I can. I am.
Or am I a new man: an American?

To my river, the Susquehanna,
I look and wave good-bye.
This once it answers back:
Don't forget me.
In the wee hours of a sleepy town
I hop a semi pre-arranged
and wake up
in the dawn looking at the GWB and NYC.

Where do the Hudson and Harlem flow?

II.
STATE

Imagining the Johnstown Flood

After the W.A. Rodgers illustration from Harper's Weekly

One hundred years later, the picture
seems so overdone. The sepia-toned

woman—empty arms outstretched like
Longfellow's Evangeline grasping

for Gabriel—reaches toward her
bearded husband, child in a dressing

gown. The tattered family clinging
to a cracked roof. The stuff

of melodrama. Giant splinters
of trees, houses, furnishings,

wagons, a perambulator. A face
of one already passed, looking

up from beneath and beyond.
And everywhere the water. Waves.

Rain. Surges. Surges. Surges.
Yet look closer. Bring your eyes

down from the steep cliffs that still
line the Conemaugh Valley, away from

the 20 million tons of torrent
sweeping south from the broken dam.

Come away from the twin
church steeples, all that's left

of the Lord's place.
Come back to her. Someone younger

than you are now. With ten short fingers
and two vacant eyes.

This Is Where It Comes From

Tires whir on the flat road as the odometer clicks
off Florida a tenth of a mile at a time. It is
cool in the rental car. We have been at Marco

A week, drinking drinks on the sand, acting coy. The day
is overcast, and it will rain around 2, the concierge
confides. I take them for a ride. In the back seat,

Rita repeats the story of the overbearing Philadelphia
man we met at the beach yesterday. "What a card,"
she says. "What a card." Charlie laughs again.

Reciting from the AAA book, Beth runs down the list
of tonight's restaurant choices. I drive on as the soil
shifts from pale sand to light brown earth. Irrigation
                canals

Separate huge rectangles of land like long, narrow
ribbons of blue-brown water. We pass acres and
acres of orange groves where fat trees bearing fat fruit

Are lined up in perfect, perfect rows. Behind
ten-foot high chain link fences, there are endless lines
of lettuce, tomatoes, carrots, melons, cucumbers.

On the right are small square buildings with tin roofs and
sun-faded green paint. There is a large sign: Hendry
Brothers Agricultural Company. No Trespassing. It looks

Official, like something the government put there. Black
and brown bodies move slowly in the symmetrical shade.
I know who these people are—Jamaicans, Puerto Ricans,

Mexicans, Haitians, Americans. No one asks me. I
realize it will be a fifty-minute trip back to the hotel.
Rita is reading a magazine. Charlie has fallen asleep.

Beth changes the radio station. In downtown Immokalee,
hand-painted letters on plywood advertise "Soul Food—
Liquor."
The words on the other side of the street are all in
Spanish.

At the light, I match eyes with a fat old man leaning
against a rusted stake-body truck and looking at a carload
of tourists. No one is much interested. Not even him.

There Is Only One Show Business

It all means something.
Why go for quality? I spit.
More than you can imagine.

This is my last jacket.
On the floor. On the next
a man handing out New Testaments.

Good news from. Misheard.
Holy Moley. In my day.
It was night. Morning soon.

The Civil War: Gettysburg
Fought over shoes. 60,000
souls float. To heaven.

My second to last . . . Dance.
Like pistons, toes tapped.
Forced wood to give way.

In the forties, 400 lost.
A woman saved. Thrown out
the window. Things end

And go on. Why keep it?
Cloth like this. A dime.
When it meant something.

Unearned

A woman—young—a girl really:
sitting on the false concrete
outside Tizz Club. Brown-red dreadlocks
dip across drooping eyes. Vulnerable—
a thin jacket —she can't gauge the weather.

Unfold her legs. A muted green
Chinese dragon on a brown-red
calf. Bitter strength and peacefulness
is its motto. This is a rough
translation. My hand: unguided.

There is a moon-blue mountain on
the left edge of the horizon:
It is possibility.
The mountain is grounded by
brown-red rocks and earth. A terse end.

The girl gets up to leave. I can't
accept this. You would not either.
A dog howls into the brown-red
fire glowing: across the town,
across night. Birds sing lovely songs.

Nearly Every Time

Whistle low, moans across
The prairie. A woman in a heavy

Brown dress, brown hat, looks
Out, sees three buffalo. Screech

Almost unheard into Penn Station,
1945, when the war was ours.

The clack of Negro porters' heels.
The tap of old ladies' shoes

Switching from front to back
As they cross the line. Smoke

Across Ohio, returning Lincoln
To Illinois. Dropping quarters,

Watching *Donahue* on a little pay
Screen in 30th Street Station,

Philadelphia. The boy with
The pillowcase suitcase, Harrisburg,

1978. The smiling, greasy engineman
Pulling the first up the grade, out

Of Scranton, Steamtown, U.S.A.
Smoking at the black and white arm,

Listening to the steady rhythm of a mile's
Worth of box cars. The overnight ride

To Miami, 1948, when swamps were still
Swamps. In the club car, the woman coughs

Into her handkerchief. Accepts a drink from
A man in a white shirt. Nods in acknowledgment.

It Goes On

For Richard Hugo
the poet of the Duwamish

I might come to your house some Sunday,
say my life's broke down. Tell you my wife's
half crazy, that the kids have less respect
than dogfish, just watch TV all day.

I'll go to your kitchen, open the fridge,
drink your beer. Talk you into doing vodka
shots from those little antique rose glasses
while Tony's pizza slices warm in the toaster oven.

I might get real drunk, hazy, but you'd
feel it, too. And we'd call up a couple
of girls and walk to meet them at Sidler's
tavern in what's left of downtown.

And I might put a whole five spot
in the jukebox and strum the pool cue
and twirl it like my rifle at Parris Island and
never think about how the only people

Who learn twirling are grunts and majorettes.
And when the slow song comes on, that one
from years ago, and the girl, my one,
asks to dance, I might just move my boots.

Three to a Frame

At 3 o'clock in the morning
my wife is in a swimming pool,
giant as a lake.
The water is warm, but not
too much so.
She is swimming and swimming,
twirling like one of those women
in that new Olympic event.
She is really having a good time.

I'm at the bottom of the pool
on a Barcolounger in full recline,
looking up from a book.
I appear startled,
she says.

There is a special emptiness
in a bowling alley at 1:37 on a week day.
The kids aren't out of school yet,
over here playing video games.
Mavis hands me a pair of rental shoes.

This is an honest game—
candlepin—play the wood.
It is a satisfying crack that echoes
as the pins bounce off one another.
I cannot remember my dreams.

November, 1963

I.
JFK ruined it,
walking down Pennsylvania Avenue,
hatless, in 20-degree January.
Standing on the platform next to him,
Eisenhower,
with his Khrushchev face,
forced to doff his top,
revealed the bald lie of the fifties.
Even LBJ had to take his hat off
to shade Frost's poetry.

Now we are all
uncovered, unprotected.
Our sons don't know how
to wear hats.
They wear caps, backwards,
ignorant of our loss. Unknowing,
they remind us of Roy Campanella
squatting, squinting into the afternoon
sun at Ebbets Field.
Of how we left Campy, alone and
crippled, in the empty bleachers
of Brooklyn.

The rest of us
remain hatless.
Or pretend. Don some
musty felt fedora, but
it's only a remembrance,
out of place now.
All because JFK
rode hatless, topless,
through the streets of Dallas.

II.
Old Joe knew the pain
when Joe Jr. exploded somewhere
over the continent. Bits of metal,

Cloth and blood raining down
from sky to soil. The unexpected
sacrifice exacted by ambition. You

Would know it, too. Pacing the
tiled floor in Children's Hospital
while Patrick is pulled, five weeks

Early and impermanent, from Jackie's
womb. *In nomine Patris et Filii
et Spiritus Sancti.* "He wouldn't take

His hands off that little coffin.
I was afraid he'd carry it right
out with him," Cardinal Cushing said.

We did it for you. Out into the streets
of America. We shared your sadness.
But that sorrow was only a primer.

III.
I got out
of the Army that morning
and was glad to be going home
for Thanksgiving, for good.
On Route 15, hitchhiking
to save money,
a farmer in a blue pick-up
stopped for me three miles
outside Gettysburg. Told me
the news. Didn't say another word.
Just dropped me off in Carlisle.

Lot's Kingdom

Unaided, rumor hung thick
Like a heavy-clouded night sky.

Those who were once ours stalled,
Became a low, stagnant front.

But not us. He, sharp
As winter wind,

Had us sailing like corks
Wafting in the blue.

But by the approach
Of the second eve

I heard it, too. The deacon
Has a niece, one said

And nodded with air of kith.
The sun painted the sky with rouge

Watercolors. By morning
Only half remained in the campaign.

The wind was turning. My fingers
Scaled the air; I knew

Not whether to go or stay.

In the Land of the Iroquois

Thomas,

I am in despair. The noise
From the trains keeps me up all night.
It's an incessant clacking,

Like the railroad cars are running
Over the body of Abraham Lincoln.
I am drinking again. Inappropriate

Things. A Bloody Mary at midnight,
Cordials in the morning. The sweet
Taste lingers, taxing my mouth all day.

Oh for a gin and tonic. Quinine
Would get rid of it. There are
Caterpillars here. Big ones,

A foot long like the hot dog.
I want to kill them, but can't
Bring myself to do it. Instead

I classify them using the Bertillon method,
Knowing they'll return to the scene.
I know I am missing the season.

Sometimes I feel just like a plant.
It's late, and because we are without
The benefit of clergy they would ask

Us to go. Still things are favorable
For those of georgic virtue. My specimens
Should take first prize in tomorrow's

Bench show. I'll trouble you no longer,
Just remember that in this edition
The words in red are said to be those of Christ.

Regards,

Jeremy

It's That Season Again

Yesterday, three bishops of the Roman Catholic Church
            walked
down North Pleasant Street in full Advent regalia. Once,
            one lifted
me just two inches off the ground, then ran out of fuel.

Gaugin is among us. Late or early as usual. Chuck Berry,
            too.
My opinions are always in the majority. These little yellow
trucks have such an amiable aesthetic quality.

The Astrologist

Not in your town. Me
Out of mine. Yet, to each
His own. In stars, time. Gifts

For giving. A treat to be
A little king. Coarse cloth.
Smell. This earthly place.

Now yours. Welcome. Oh,
Something missing? Listen to
Our dream. Then flee. But remember:

Three. And then an odd one

Out means consequences. Always.
We are princes, Chaldics set to stars.
You, the little King of kings.

Nally's Autumn at Nauset Light

Grandpa howls like a coyote
in the darkness. *Olagon, Olagon* he cries
in Irish tones. I bring medicine.

He asks for whiskey. Once awake,
he curses the beasts in the scrub pine.
The Audubon man says probably

Three families of them, living
on rabbits and stray dogs.
They seem displaced on the dunes

Of Nauset. Each day Grandpa grows
more difficult, demanding things
that I cannot give. That no one can give.

He believes he is the last, *begorro,*
all the others have gone. He
refuses Florida, begrudgingly accepts

The little help I can offer.
Three times a week I cook
eggs and sausages. We go down

To the light. He looks out over
the water. Steady as the slow
rhythm of the horn, he sees what

Is beyond seeing. A nod, and
we head to the car. The way
home is always the same.

Half a Mile Off Everglades City, Florida

The water is shallow here.
A good-sized man,
finding himself and his boat
tipped over, could stand
and walk to the mangrove shore.
No gators in the salt to bother
you, but don't do it
on the inside of the bay
where sets of floating eyes
scour the surface
looking for a mistake.

The water is shallow here
and warm as a bath. Piss-warm,
warm as a can of beer left out
in the afternoon sun.
March winds don't reach
down this far. No one
has to say it:
This is as far as you can go
and remain unchanged.

The water is shallow,
yet big fish swim in it.
Fish big as a hog.
Big as those tawny,
one-hump cows standing
in the pine-dotted pastures
a mile inland. Those lonesome
cows forced to keep
tick-eating snow-white egrets
as companions.

The water the color of a faded emerald.
The Park Service tourist boat
cuts through it as the engine spits.

The smell of brine and mildewed
life preservers drips down
the back of your throat
like uncut cocaine.

A pelican dives and finds his dinner
in it. Translucent shrimp tickle
the inside of his pouch. A cormorant,
black as the Big Cypress Swamp at midnight,
finds a perch and spreads his wings to dry.
Over a crackling speaker, a sun-bleached
guide, dressed in the standard—khaki shirt
and faded jeans—drones on.

The water is shallow here.
And pure and clear.
Eight miles out it touches the sky.
The sky is so clear
that it may be possible
to look right past Mexico,
all the way around the world,
and see the Holy St. John
dipping Jesus into deep blue
waters of the River Jordan.

I Am Sober as a Sandwich

I could have been a carnie. Short-changing
Kids. Sucking in hicks, out on their annual date
With Lulubelle, too dumb to know the difference

Between cents and sense. Instead I'm steam-pressing
Rich guys' trousers. Listening to Gloria Simmons
Whine about the pleats her round butt

Is just gonna push right out anyhow.
I could have been a carnie. Knew a man once,
Owned one of them shows. There I'd be working

My way through Indiana and Ohio from April
To October. Sapping a drunk on our last night in town,
Scoring an extra fifty. You're a businessman, my daddy
        says.

It's true. But oh to be driving a truck with a camper.
Maybe towing a trailer full of Games O' Chance
And cheap toys full of newspaper

Stuffing. Smoking butts like there's no hell. Going back
To Florida each winter. Getting drunk. Getting stoned.
Fighting. Fighting. Fighting.

Yeah, I could have been a carnie. I probably wouldn't
Have gotten a tattoo. At 25, I would have found religion.
Found a regular job. Married a Christian girl. But only if

I had worked the carnie. At least then I'd have some
        stories
To tell around the campfire on the Men's Group
weekend retreats after the Reverend Johnson goes to
        sleep.

The Girl with the Red Guitar

I.
Rosewood.
My hands are teak.
I place my fingers in my ears.
I can still hear her E
sharp or flat.
I do not know.
I am not trained musically.

II.
Vibrato.
Little, little, little tremors.
In my head.
Her imagination takes over,
overtakes me.
A kind of kind.
I see you understand.

A Cloud in Cantonese

He was the "Russell Wong" of my high school.
He smelled like a man. And when I smelled

Him, my life was changed.
I asked him if he had feeling for me.

He said, "Yes," but I, too, must show respect.
"Do not embarrass me to the *dai lo,*" he said.

"Step away when I speak to my brothers."
He was brave and had much power.

"The new order is the young order,"
He told me. "These men are old

And do not realize the consequence."
Sometimes he would go to New York,

Toronto, or another city. Sometimes
I think he will not come back.

Before I knew him I was a shy girl.
My friends try to make date for me,

Tell me I am pretty. That this boy
Or that one like me. I refuse.

After I meet him I become two people:
First I am passion, like the moon.

I hunger for his light to shine.
But also I am a cloud floating in the corner.

I felt like an ant, lifting my heart
Many times my weight. I cried into

The spring, until autumn.
When I see him walking, riding

In the car, I feel shame because
He does not notice me.

All this I felt, until yesterday.

Standing in Line at the Purity Supreme

I remember that girl,
I think to myself
standing in line at the Purity Supreme.
I remember her.
Her hair was long back then
and dark as a moonless night.

I remember her eyes,
bright and friendly,
the way the harbor lights look
to Portuguese fisherman
after seven days at sea.

I remember the summer
when we were too young to drive.
We walked everywhere,
mostly out to the dunes by Skinner's Beach.
We'd sit on the damp sand for hours,
talk and hold hands.
And back then it was enough.

She's not that girl,
standing in a checkout line
on a Wednesday after work.
She's a woman
with a hint of gray and the weary
look of a commuter.

We don't speak.
Perhaps she doesn't remember,
or maybe she's embarrassed
by what we have become.

She's a woman
like so many others
in a boiled-wool jacket

and photos of her kids tucked
among the credit cards
in her wallet.

And me a man.
Like so many others.
Standing in the express line
in a wrinkled shirt
and a tie that almost matches
with two microwave dinners,
some fruit, and an uncertain gaze.

In a Perfect World

You'd already be home by now.
There'd be no compact disc of Kathie Lee's favorite hits.
Todos hablaremos español.
There'd be no need for two versions of rhetoric. All night
supermarkets and bowling alleys, of course.

Each evening, citizens of small towns in the upper Plains
states and border communities in the provinces of
Saskatchewan and Manitoba would break out in a chorus
                              of "Fever."
Marching bands, marching bands. And the Chunnel.

Imagine Always Looking Up

I am a sparrow in a sky full of sparrows.
Winter flounder crowd the bottom of the harbor channel.
Dusk: the café is empty.
A damp white rag.
The smell of gasoline makes us dizzy.
For an instant I am grasping the bar
of the carousel horse. It moves. Disappears.

My wings stiffen in the cold. Tender. Like glue.

Department of Defense

We'd been to the club to hear
Louie strum guitar, sing,

"It was all clear. You were
meant to be here," while we

huddled in our maroon vinyl booth
on the cusp of our first separation.

Near two a.m., we pull into the Kwik-Stop
to get gas. My ship leaves at 5.

Me and 4,999 brothers aboard
a four and a half acre flattop

for a late summer cruise.
A flex of our NATO commitment.

Grace goes into the store to buy
some gum. A steady thump echoes

across the street to the pumps.
"Disco Jam Tonight" on a sign out front,

cheap plastic letters surrounded by red
and green blink lights.

Fun funk, but something's not right.
I see the woman first, gold shiny slinky dress

running across six lanes of traffic
in the cool VA Beach dampness.

She is drunk, and carrying
a twelve-inch butcher knife.

But he's already next to me, pursued and
breathing hard. Grabs a nozzle. Threatens

to flick his Bic. "I'll kill us all,"
he says. For an instant I am torn.

Not often are choices made so clear.
Leave now, and leave Grace behind?

Opening the car door, I motion
for her to hustle.

Weeks later, off Norway, in the green
light of the late watch, the boys and I

slap box to break the boredom.
Bodies move against the rhythm

of the music from the boom box.
Dewayne's fingers slide across my

brow as I feign a hit to his gut.
We code the now old story, say,

"Ha, disco jam tonight."

Six Views of Stevie

I.
With a basketball,
always a basketball,
bouncing, bouncing.

II.
Stevie in his blue VW Bug,
parked at the river,
rolling joints.
Spitting out tiny seeds.
The tape deck plays
"There is a town in north Ontario."
Stevie believes, sings along.

III.
Stevie puts on the weighted
vest. In the alley, he jumps
100 times. 200 times.
After every ninth jump,
he says, "One more for Jesus,"
just for fun. He casts a shadow
on the green garage door.

IV.
The mother gives up.
The father says "dummy."
Stevie still skips class.
He goes to the recruiting man.
Then he goes away.

V.
He has bad teeth
because he has no money.
He has no money.

VI.

Stevie is ten. Eating ice cream.
Everybody likes him, except
Mr. Harris, who saw Stevie
breaking windows in
our old gold ghost house.

Happy Hour

Delight in your youth, young man, make the most of your early days; let your heart and your eyes show you the way; but remember that for all these things God will call you to account.

—Ecclesiastes 11:9

Stevie, my friend
since second grade, raises
a glass, makes a toast:
    We are still young, aren't we?
Yes, I try to tell him,   but know
the untruth.   Stevie thinks of ball
fields, of a pitch or a pass.
Those places have been plowed under.

    I've spent half my time,
wasting my desire.
      Resisting no
temptation until I have
no temptation left.
My lungs blackened, I cough
at the mirror, out the window.
I've pissed myself,
my bed. Soiled
myself with beer-sauced bowels.
Used women like fool's money.
    Once, one was to have a child,
    then scraped it away.
I did not pay for this.

I have no house. The farm
bought and sold.
My share a car in a ditch.
Lamentation is my legacy,
a regret of no regret   for no one.
Yet I have done things

safe men never dreamed.
Taken and given
love,
aggravation,
mercy,
fear.

I've lent a hand to strangers.
    Had a pool cue across my face,
a blade to my back. Known fidelity, forgiveness
by name, and the color of kindness.
I've left jobs when it pleased.
Found money the quick, hard way.

Sung songs, to women, and rivers
and friends.   And to myself.
(Such a sweet melody I can sing to myself.)
    And so, Stevie, I say this is enough,
but not nearly.

Todos Son Contra Mí

It's a beautiful day;
the birds fly upside-down
like seals imitating Laplanders
swimming in the bay.

If I were not perfectly sure of my ability
to create a new taxonomy
out of these strange dichotomies,
then I'd rather live in a swamp.

Consider the lilies of the field
And James Brown still in jail.
50,000 white folks can't be wrong.
Justice, never pale.

I grew up around here.
I fell down over there.
So small I was just mere.
In Spanish, they say *Al Que Quiere.*

Plowing the Mule on These 40 Acres

In memory of James Byrd, Jr.

You say it's about the past, about making
up for something somebody's ancestors did years
ago: ancient history. I wish it were. I'd let it slide.

I'm talking about being six damn years old, and being
                    chased
down Walnut Street, in Sunbury, PA, past my aunt's
                    house,
right down Furman's alley and up to the steps by two
                    white

Teenagers with sticks yelling, "Nigger, go home." And
                    seeing
my German great-grandmother and whipping past her
                    and wondering,
"Ain't I already home?" I'm talking about my
                    grandmother

Dropping nine-year-old me off at a barbershop in Lee
                    County,
Florida, (yes, that Lee) and when she comes back from
                    grocery shopping
I'm still sitting, unsheared, in that same chair, and
                    the cracker barber

Tells her, "I ain't never cut no colored's hair and I ain't
                    fixing to start."
After that my stepfather cut my hair with one of those
                    cheap-ass
devices you get at Woolworth's and he always did a piss-
                    poor job.

I'm talking about being in middle school and that wise
                    guy
kid who sat at my table saying, "Half-breed, who put
the cream in your coffee?" and the teacher, blonde, pretty

Mrs. Jensen, snickering and telling the kid to keep quiet.
I'm talking about sitting in a corner reading books on my
                    own
throughout most of middle school and each quarter
                    collecting

D's for "dummy" and C's for "couldn't care less" and
                    when
the end of eighth grade rolls around and those state test
                    scores
come back placing me at the top in a few categories, my
                    social

Studies teacher comes to me to express surprise that I am
"intelligent." I'm talking about not having a date for the
                    prom
because the girl who asked me came back a few days later

Explaining that her father wouldn't let her go. I'm talking
                    about
Having a woman in church—my church where I had my
                    baptism,
first communion, confirmation—moving her purse to her
                    left side

When I sat eight feet to her right. That day while
                    listening
to the Lord's Prayer, the "forgive us our trespasses" part
became clear. I'm talking about having to show two

forms of ID in the Sears in the Independence Mall in
                    Kingston,

Massachusetts, and while waiting in line noticing that
none of the white/right customers had to whip out their

DriverslicenselibrarycardemployeeIDselectiveserviceregis-
trationpassport.
I'm talking about all those Klan membersympathizers
with their neo-confederate
flags flying proudly from the front bumper. I'm talking
about serving my country,

Your country, our country, and being stationed in
Virginia Beach
and being refused admission to a night club after some
white guys
go in front of me. And stupid me, sitting home two
hours later that night

Watching TV when it finally hits me why I couldn't get
into that club.
I'm talking about being a college professor and the
woman calling to enroll her
daughter in my summer creative writing course saying to
me,

"This area is much nicer than Virginia because there aren't
so many—
ummm—minorities." And me not saying a thing, but
making a point
to introduce myself a few weeks later at the Parents'
Night reading.

I'm talking about every day I wake up and think I look
black, and that
means I am black and that means I better watch what I
do. Yeah, because
sometimes I sit around thinking I've made it, that my
mother, rest her soul,

Would be proud. Then I think, "Made what? How come
            the only other
dark face I see all day is that of the janitor?" I'm talking
            about
keeping my son's baseball bat at the top of the cellar steps

In case some day some Klan idiot decides he and his
            buddies
don't like no germanafrican being married to an
            irishfrench and comes to visit.
Do not say no. It has happened, it does happen, it will
            happen.

Friend, I'm talking about today.

Epilogue

An Opening

Here on the pulse of this new day
You may have the grace to look up and out
                    — Maya Angelou

Put your hand on this substandard, subhuman,
subliminal, subterranean subway bench.
Place it palm down. Now hit it with a hammer, hard.
Put a nail through it, maybe two.
Stupid, huh? Baby, you've been
doing worse for years.

Yes, there is only one answer
and if I tell it to you,
you will hear it, but you
will not know it. So what's
the point in telling you, you know?

OK, you've earned it.   Step right
up and off the page.   Watch
your head, low ceilings.
(That roof needs razing.)
And watch your first step . . . And

the second, third, 42nd, 59th, 86th,
125th.   No Japalac or Tintex on this line.
This here's the heart, dear heart. The real deal.
So when you see
somebody seeing you, say hello.   And
when you see somebody knowing you

     reach out your hand, grasp firmly and say,

          "Good morning."

Acknowledgments

Grateful acknowledgment is made to the following publications, in which these poems, some in earlier versions, first appeared:

The Cape Codder: "Nally's Autumn at Nauset Light,"
   "Standing in Line at the Purity Supreme"
Fan: a Baseball Magazine: "#39"
5 AM: "Imagining the Johnstown Flood"
Forkroads: A Journal of Multi-Ethnic American Literature:
   "Susquehanna Song"
The Literary Network News: "The Astrologist"
Mudville Diaries: A Book of Baseball Memories: "#39"
*Mulberry Poets & Writers Association 1998 Poetry
   Daybook:* "The Girl With the Red Guitar"
Old Crow: "This Is Where It Comes From"
The Pittsburgh Post-Gazette: "An April Funeral in
   Pennsylvania"
West Branch: "Sailor Boy in the Checker Bar on Maundy
   Thursday Night"

About the Author

Jerry Wemple grew up in central Pennsylvania and southwestern Florida. He served in the United States Navy and later worked as a newspaper reporter in Massachusetts. He holds a Bachelor of Arts degree from Vermont College and a Master of Fine Arts in English from the University of Massachusetts, Amherst.

After an absence of many years, Jerry has returned to his native Susquehanna Valley in Pennsylvania where he lives with his wife, Deirdre Galvin, and their children, Kyle and Jamila. He teaches at Bloomsburg University.

He is a recipient of a fellowship in literature from the Pennsylvania Council on the Arts. *You Can See It from Here*, seventh annual winner of the Naomi Long Madgett Poetry Award, is his first published collection.